You can contact the author by email on:
thegreenhubinfo@gmail.com
Twitter: @ighodaloh
Instagram: @ighodaloh
and on Facebook.

ACKNOWLEDGMENTS

First of all, I acknowledge the Almighty God for His incredible love and grace upon my life, for it is in Him I move, breathe and have my being. All I am today and becoming is because of Him.

I want to thank the former President of Nigeria, His Excellency, Dr. Goodluck Ebele Jonathan for being such an inspiration and beacon of hope to millions of children across the globe. For letting his story inspire countless people and being a true statesman and Africa's hero of democracy.

Thanks to Ejovwoke Okorodafe for putting flesh to the story I passionately wanted to tell and giving it life, you made all the difference dear. To Segun Victor Ayo, I say a very big thank you for contributing illustrations to this piece. Also to Sunday Zuoke, thank you for final touches and pre-press proofing. I also thank Siloko Siasia; I'm grateful for all the help you rendered.

To Umachiyam and Uwethu Odukwu, thank you for being a source of inspiration to writing and development of this book.

Finally, I will not fail to thank my brother Oseyomon Ushor who is always a major source of inspiration and drive, for always beleiving in me and being a great brother. Thanks to my mentors, friends and family. God bless you all.

To every African child out there, especially the less privileged ones living poor; be hopeful and hold on to your beautiful dreams. You will achieve all your dreams with time.

DEDICATION

This book is dedicated to every African child with a dream; a dream to make Africa great.

Believe in yourself because you can achieve those dreams.

Oseyomon Ighodaloh

CONTENTS

GUIDE TO ILLUSTRATIONS

CHAPTER 1

A Good Start

Goodluck loved the way she stroked his head tenderly but also wanted to go back to his game of hide and seek with his friends.

G oodluck! Goodluck!" "Yes Mama!" The reply came swiftly as the young lad ran to his mother. Ma Jonathan looked up at her son from her small kitchen stool where she sat inspecting the fishes which she would sell at the market.

"My Goodman!" she exclaimed "look how tall you are. You are even taller than I am"

Goodluck smiled broadly, revealing his fine white dentition, a good contrast for his dark skin. He was used to his mother's sweet tease and loved the way she fondly called him her "Goodman".

"Mama, you know that because you are on a stool" He replied as he squat beside her. "You see, now who is taller?"

"My Goodman" She pat his head softly with admiration in her eyes. "You've grown so fast and it seems you were born just yesterday".

Ma Jonathan smiled as she recalled sweet memories. It was the 20th of November, 1957. Oh how excited she was at the birth of her boy child, that cool Wednesday evening. As the village midwife laid him in her arms, she was overcome with joy. A joy that did not spring from the traditional value of male children in Africa; it was the pure joy of a mother who had received a priceless gift from God with contentment. Pa Jonathan, equally as proud and content, named him "Goodluck". A family like theirs needed lots of it and some luck would see them through each day of their poor lives. He also inherited his father's name – Ebele Jonathan. Another son had been born into otuoke village of the Ogbia community, another kinsman. As ma Jonathan looked at him now, she placed the chubby little boy in her memory along side this fast growing lad, measuring the progress which was indeed great; so great that Ma Jonathan was sure it was time for her son to start school. He was six years old going on seven and stood at almost four feet. Surely it was time she thought to herself. But supposing Pa Jonathan objected to it? As his only son, he was expected to learn the family trade of making canoes and fishing. The boy had already begun to learn a thing or two about canoe carving and pa Jonathan would no doubt be looking forward to the time when Goodluck would be able to help in the family business. All the possibilities made her thoughts drift away and she might have continued her daydreams, had her son not jolted her out of it.

"Mama, I'm here, you called me" Goodluck loved the way she stroked his head tenderly but he also wanted to go back to his game of hide and seek with his friends.

"Yes I called you. Stand here in front me" Goodluck left Ma Jonathan's side and stood before her.

"Now put your hand over your head and touch your ear" she watched as he obeyed. "Don't bend your head, hmmm, like that" she smiled. Yes, surely it was time for her son to go to school for this was the way children qualified to start their education in the 1960s.

"Mama, see my hand has reached! Does that mean I get to attend school?" asked a wide eyed, excited Goodluck. Even he did not notice how tall he now was.

"Yes my dear, you shall go to school. You see, I told you how tall you were just now eh? And I was right". Some excitement danced in her eyes for a moment followed by worry as she thought of the money required for school fees and everything else Goodluck would need. She had her meager savings but that would not go all the way. However, she had resolved that her son must be educated.

"Mama, can I drop my hand now?" Goodluck still stood with hand over head. Ma Jonathan laughed as she told him he could go back to his game. But he was not to tell anyone this news until he talked to Pa Jonathan. Goodluck dashed off as quickly as he had come in and Ma Jonathan watched him leave until she stared into space. Goodluck, totally oblivious of his mother's thoughts and fears, continued in the game outside. Ma Jonathan listened to the soothing sound of their innocent and exciting laughter as they sang happily. It echoed through the yard, slowly fading as they ran into the bushes.

I will find your hiding place!

I will find your hiding place!

Up in the tree or down in the bushes!

I will find your hiding place!

One, two, three, four, five, six, seven, eight, nine, ten!

And with that, the seekers went off to find those in hiding. One of the seekers nearly bumped into Goodluck's older sister, Obebatein, as she carried a pail of water on her head to her mother.

"Watch it!" She yelped as she got out of the way just in time. When she got to the kitchen, she set down the water. "Mama, these children nearly knocked me down and..." she paused as she noticed the dreamy look in Ma Jonathan's eyes. "Mama, what are you thinking about?"

Ma Jonathan shrugged, looked up at her and smiled. "A good beginning" she replied with no further explanation, and she turned to her basket of fishes. Obebatein, though curious, quietly joined her till their task was done.

CHAPTER 2

Goodluck Goes To School

Goodluck stood at the old school gate staring

Goodluck's first day at school finally came and he was excited. He woke up early enough to watch the sunrise that beautiful Monday morning, so he could do his chores and get ready in time for school. He swept their thatched house with a broom of twigs, removed the cobwebs and fetched some water from the village stream; his mother would not hear of his being lazy or neglecting his duties, neither would his father who believed in working hard to earn a living and a good name. Besides that, Goodluck considered his going to school a privilege

He told his mother and sister all about school

and wanted to do his best from the start. Pa Jonathan had planned for him to learn fishing and canoe carving to support the family and Goodluck had almost lost hope of ever going to school, even though he admired other children who attended. Thank God Ma Jonathan persuaded him gently, insisting that she could bear the burden of his fees and that God would provide. Pa Jonathan finally gave in, no longer able to deny his wife's request. And so, on this Monday as the sun rose in its bright yellow glory, Goodluck was dressed and ready for school. Ma Jonathan was also awake and she made certain her son took all that he needed; at least, all they could afford. He wore his school uniform – a clean pair of shorts and a shirt, with one notebook tucked under his arm and a pencil in his pocket. He had no school bag on his back or shoes on his feet because they could not afford to buy any.

"My Goodman, you look ready to go" Ma Jonathan said, patting his head as she always did. Please always focus on your lessons and listen to the teacher. I have such faith that you will do well"

Then she prayed to God to guide her son aright and give him understanding and wisdom so that they would be proud of him. Off Goodluck went, down the village path that led to St. Stephen's primary school, Otuoke. As he strolled bare footed in steady strides, every tree and shrub on the pathway seemed to dance and wave happily at him as though all of nature shared in his joy that day.

It was 7:30 am and Goodluck stood at the old, squeaky, school gate, staring at the broken down school gate, staring at the broken sign board which once had the words St. Stephen's Primary School, Otuoke written boldly in blue; now it read imary School Otuk. Goodluck didn't mind, to him it was just a white wooden board with dusty blue lines on it. Soon, I'll learn to read he thought to himself as he walked excitedly into the small compound where he joined the gathering assembly. Everything was new to Goodluck – the short, straight lines formed by the pupils as they stood according to their classes, the national anthem which the students yelled at the top of their voices and of course the stern looking grown ups who were their teachers. Goodluck felt a bit out of place when he saw that a few pupils had shiny rubber sandals on their feet. But some others were also bare footed like him, so he didn't let it bother him. The headmaster addressed the assembly, encouraging the pupils to work hard to excel in their studies. When he concluded, the pupils marched off to their classes, singing a song raised by a teacher. The classrooms were in a hall divided into three parts making primary one, two and three. The school had no primary four to six classes because the pupils were too few for the provision of more classes. There were five pupils in each class, making fifteen in the entire school. Goodluck was in primary one and when their lessons started, he listened with kin interest as they studied the alphabet and numbers. At the end of their lessons, their class teacher Mr. Olu, gave them some homework and dismissed the class. Mr. Olu came from the western region of Nigeria, Ogun state. He came to the part of Rivers State – now known as Bayelsa state – to teach at the primary school and dwell among the Ijaw people. It was quite a distance from home, but he grew to love the lifestyle of the people which revolved around fishing and farming. Mr. Olu left the classroom with his books in his hand and the pupils followed. The sun was high and the ground felt like hot coals as Goodluck walked home. He was glad when he got to their thatched house and he greeted his parents happily, before going in to take a bath and change his clothes. He told his mother and Obebatein all about school as they relaxed in the backyard after lunch. Ma Jonathan listened patiently with a smile on her face. Although she didn't understand everything he said, she loved the sound of it. Goodluck had just concluded his report, when his good friend Benson Agadaga, who lived two compounds away, came to visit. He too received a fresh account of Goodluck's experience; like ma Jonathan he listened attentively without understanding it all but hoped he would go to school like his friend. Benson's parents were poor just like Goodluck's and they could not afford to send him to school that year.

"Don't worry Benson" His father had told him "I promise to send you to school next year. You hear?"

As he listened now to an excited Goodluck, he prayed in his heart that his father would make good his promise.

CHAPTER 3

"If you lose a tooth..."

Salaam Alaikum Mohammed

It was a Friday afternoon and Goodluck was in his room going through his weekend assignments. His attendance at school was just two weeks now but Mr. Olu was not going to slow down on homework – not even for a fresher. He wanted all his pupils to be hard working and focused. Goodluck was not going to disappoint him because those were his treasured virtues. He looked at the papers over and over again, as he sat on his local hand woven mat with bamboo underneath. It was hard and uncomfortable but had grown used to it and even felt content to dive onto it after a tiring day. When he was done with one paper, he felt it was time to take a break. He and Benson planned to pick shells that afternoon for counting lessons at school. He walked to the sitting room and looked at the old pendulum clock on the muddy wall.

"I wonder he's not here yet" Goodluck said under his breadth. As he turned to go back to his room, he heard his friend's voice outside. Benson was greeting Goodluck's mother and sister who were seated at the small veranda, dressing the vegetables which they would cook for lunch. After Goodluck told Ma Jonathan where they were going, they set out for the river with spring steps. They talked on the way and laughed aloud when they recalled anything amusing. They had nearly reached their destination when they saw Mohammed walking towards them. Benson spotted him first and called out.

"Salaam Halekum, mohammed!"

"Salaam Ma-le-ku, Benson" He replied stressing each syllable of the last word in a bid to correct Benson's mistake. This Arabic greeting was common among Muslims and this was Mohammed's religion. His family moved from the North to Bayelsa three years ago and it seemed they had come to stay.

"Mallam, Salaam Maleku" Goodluck also greeted

"Maleku salaam, Goodluck" Mohammed smiled from ear to ear as he got to where they stood. He found it amusing that Goodluck called him "mallam" and he loved the way these two identified with him by greeting in Arabic; it made him feel happy and accepted. Some other kids made fun of Mohammed because he was Hausa and a Muslim; but not Goodluck and Benson. They loved the little dark skinned boy, with chocolate brown eyes and an oblong shaped head decorated with black curls. Benson lived next to Mohammed and the two families were in good terms.

"Going to the river?" He asked

"Yes, to pick some shells. Want to come?" Benson offered.

"Thank you, maybe some other time. I have to get home now. Bye" Mohammed trotted away, clanking his old metal bucket.

"Nice chap" Goodluck told Benson as they continued walking.

"Yes, pity they might move soon"

"Move?" Goodluck was surprised.

"I heard his father telling my parents this morning that they may go back to the north, where it's safer" Benson explained. There had been reports on the radio of the unrest in the East and North of Nigeria. The two regions recently had violent clashes because there was no trust among the Hausas and Igbos. It seemed it was now better to be in one's own land.

"They are such nice people, I hope they never leave" Said Goodluck. "I don't care where they are from"

"Me too" Benson agreed.

They got to the river where some villagers were busy about their affairs. Women were washing, men were fishing and young boys dived in and out of the shallow parts of the river. It was a fine place. The plants were fresh and green and birds chirped beautiful melodies high up in the surrounding trees. Benson and Goodluck

"I think you have five laps to go", his sister was enjoying the sport.

picked all the shells they needed, putting them into a little bag. There were all sorts – periwinkle shells, oyster shells and snail shells. On their way back from the river, they saw a big mango tree with some ripe fruits.

"Hey!" Benson exclaimed, his eyes twinkling with delight. "Ripe mangoes! Wonder why we didn't notice before. And so many too!" He imagined eating one of them, the thought made his stomach rumble. Up he went, climbing with agility. He hung upside down from a branch to amuse himself a little before he began plucking and throwing down mangoes to Goodluck who was on the ground. When he was done, he slowly came down from the tree and they packed up to leave. Benson took one last look at the tree and spotted another ripe juicy mango he had missed.

"Look at that fat juicy one" He pointed

Goodluck also saw it and suggested they use a stone to knock it down. The boys looked for stones, aimed at the fruit and threw. The mango dropped after a few throws but a fairly large stone also came down with it.

"Ow!" Goodluck yelled, as he quickly dropped the mango he had caught, and put his hand to his mouth.

"Sorry. What is it? Are you hurt?" Benson asked, trying to see where the stone had hit.

"My teeth" Goodluck said softly and he bared his teeth which were now a light colour.

"You're bleeding. I'm sorry about that" Benson apologized, not knowing if it was his stone or Goodluck's that caused the damage.

He ran back to the river and returned with some water in a

container of large leaves rolled in a cone. Goodluck rinsed his mouth with this a few times and all the red was gone. Then he chewed some leaves which were known for relieving pain and they walked back home.

The afternoon of the following Friday, Goodluck stood at the little wall mirror in the sitting room, with his mouth open. His incisors were gone and a huge gap remained in their place. It made him look odd and ridiculous.

"Goodluck, please come and help me get some water" Obebatein said as she walked in. when she got closer, she saw the gap in the front row. "You lost your teeth! And two of them at once" She grinned mischievously.

Goodluck appeared a little worried. "I thought it would heal and become strong again but it kept shaking loosely and as I ate some corn and pear, it came off. Sister Obebatein, do you think they will grow like finger nails do?" He called her sister before her name as a mark of respect.

Obebatein contained her laughter with great effort and tried to appear serious. "It is a rare thing for two teeth to fall at once, you know" She told Goodluck.

"Does that mean they won't grow back?" Goodluck glanced at the mirror, his worry turning to despair. Obebatein turned aside, laughed a little, then turned back to her little brother looking more serious than ever.

"Let me see". He opened up for her to take a look "Oho! You know what will make your teeth grow back?"

"What?" Goodluck was now wide eyed with hope.

"Run round the hut fourteen times and throw the teeth on the roof. Say this as you run;

If you loose a tooth it will come back

When a tooth pulls out, it will return

"I lost a tooth when I was your age and that's what I did" Obebatein smiled to show a fine set of teeth.

"Really?" Goodluck sounded a bit suspicious now.

"Really, I lost one so I ran seven times but you've lost two, so I think you'll have to double up. Never heard of a child growing a new tooth without doing it"

This was a popular practice in the 1960s and 70s. The young "tooth losers" eagerly wanted to grow back their tooth and would do anything the "wise old ones" said. Goodluck thought of it for a moment and shifting his gaze to the mirror, he saw the space; he imagined having that gap forever. No way!

"Okay, I'll go" He left the hut to begin his race. Round and round he ran, till he was panting. "Can I stop now? I'm tired" He was bent over, his hands on his knees.

"I think you have five laps to go" his sister was enjoying the sport.

Pa Jonathan who had been carving a canoe in his small work space not far from the house came home for a break, only to find his son running, sweating and chanting:

If you loose a tooth it will come back

When a tooth pulls out, it will return

He let out a hearty laugh "Goodluck, so you've lost your first tooth?" Goodluck and Obebatein who hadn't noticed his entry quickly greeted him.

"Welcome, Papa". They said together.

"Obabateeeiiin" Pa Jonathan stressed her name. "I can see your handwork"

"Papa, I have run eleven times already. Can't I throw the teeth? I don't have to run fourteen times do i?"

"Obebatein You told your brother that?" He gently scolded. "Look at him drenched in sweat." Turning to his son, he continued "Goodluck your teeth will grow back, you hear? Don't mind your sister it is an old custom; I also did it in my time but your teeth will grow even without doing it". Looking at the gap for himself, he exclaimed. "What a huge space you've got there! You lost two but expect some more soon. Don't let Obebatein trick you then too" and with that he went into the hut.

Goodluck raised an eyebrow while his sister laughed loudly. Indeed he ran the last three laps but this time, a laughing Obebatein was running too and he was close behind with a new chant:

I'll get you, I'll get you, I'll get you...

CHAPTER 4

Winning Honourably...

....his voice could be heard as he and the other pupils bellowed the anthem with pride

Time flew by so quickly and before you could say "Jack". Goodluck had almost completed his first school year. It was another beautiful Monday morning and as usual, Goodluck saw the yellow sunrise as he walked to school, its friendly rays bathing him with its warmth. He also felt warm inside each time he remembered school. He was used to the activities in class and at the assembly, his voice could be heard as he and the other pupils bellowed the anthem with pride:

Nigeria, we hail the

Our own dear native land

Though tribe and tongue may differ

In brotherhood we stand

Nigerians all and proud to serve

Our sovereign motherland

Our flag shall be a symbol

That truth and justice reign

In peace or battle honour

And this we count as gain

To pass unto our children

A banner without stain

This was the anthem up till 1978 when the patriotic music director of the Nigeria police band, Benson Odiase, wrote the melody for "Arise O compatriots..." Goodluck also knew all his classmates well. Obi was the master of trickery and his eyes always sparkled at the mere thought of mischief. Raphael was timid and always fell victim to Obi's tricks. Mr. Olu's son Ade was also in Goodluck's class and both were always in a healthy competition for first place. Sara was the only girl in the class and she was an albino. Obi teased her all the time but she paid no attention to his teasing.

Every one cheered and applauded loudly

She was one of the competitors for first place in class and got closer to clinching the crown from Ade and Goodluck who were often in a tie.

Fortunately, this Monday was another chance for a good display of academic skill because there was to be a quiz at school. Pupils from other schools in the neighbor communities were coming to Otuoke primary school to compete and there will be prizes for winners. This was the government's way of encouraging children to attend school. Goodluck hoped to win a prize.

Well who knows? I could win first place too. I have studied hard. He thought to himself as he approached the school gate. He walked into the small school hall were the quiz will take place. All St. Stephens pupils were glad there school was the venue for such an important event. When all pupils and teachers from the participating schools were present, one of the quiz judges stood up to speak. He was a tall. Huge man with bushy eye brows and a thick beard, he peered from his square shaped eye glasses as he spoke in a gentle tone. He encouraged the pupils to do their best without cheating and called on another judge to state the rules of the competition. This was a smaller man who looked like he weighed no more than a feather. He spoke quickly in voice so deep that one wondered why he had such a small neck. The rules were simple. The categories were senior, intermediate and junior. Contestants chose their questions by picking a number from the range of 1-20 and gave the number in a minute. With that, the competition was declared open and the competitors began a friendly battle of wits. They began with the senior and intermediate, before the junior category in which Goodluck had been chosen to compete. Goodluck was nervous at first, but as he progressed successfully, he gained confidence. His opponent seemed smart as he answered the questions correctly, but he didn't seem as confident. His eyes darted from left to right as though he was afraid. When they got to the final round of the contest, they gave answers to questions on history and current affairs. The teachers had already trained their pupils thoroughly on the subject.

"Master Goodluck, question 5" The judge read aloud "Who was the first prime minister of Nigeria?"

"Abubakar Tafawa Balewa" Goodluck shot back the answer.

"Two points" The judge signaled the recorder to take down the score.

"Master Peter" He addressed Goodluck's opponent "Question 8, who was made president of Nigeria in 1960?"

"Dr. Nnamdi Azikiwe" He slowly replied.

"Master Goodluck, British colonial rule in Nigeria lasted for how many years?"

"Sixty years sir, 1900-1960"

The questions and answers flew from both ends of the stage were the two participants sat all the while, Goodluck watched his opponent closely because he noticed something was amiss. When he answered his last question, he finally knew what it was.

"Who discovered quinine was a cure for malaria?" The judge asked.

Peter took a quick glance at the floor, then answered "William Baikie"

Goodluck was sure he peeped at something and he quickly told Mr. Olu who in turn told the judges. Peter and Goodluck were taken to the headmaster's office and thoroughly examined. The two boys were searched and to Goodluck's dismay, nothing implicating was found on his opponent.

"But I saw him peep into something" He gently insisted.

"You must be very careful before you accuse anyone". The headmaster looked disappointed. "The judges were going to punish you for this by taking away ten points from your score". He informed Goodluck firmly. Peter smiled while he pleaded with the headmaster.

"But sir, if ten points were deducted from my score I might not win. Please sir". He sounded close to tears but the decision was final and they went back to the hall to hear the result of the quiz. Peter won by ten points, the exact number deducted from Goodluck's score. Prizes were given, winners congratulated, and the pupils were dismissed. As the pupils left the hall, Goodluck walked slowly, looking unhappy. He had studied so hard and was so close to winning. Why had he bothered to report peter to the authorities? But surely that was the right thing to do wasn't it? As though Mr. Olu read his thoughts, he walked to Goodluck and put a hand on his shoulder.

"You did the right by telling me what you saw. I know you would never tell lies because I know you to be good boy. The most important thing you should remember is that it is always better to fail honorably than to win by cheating. Ok? The truth speaks for itself" Mr. Olu seemed to know what would happen next, for the truth began to speak in few seconds, as they watched peter dancing around to shake off soldier ants from his legs. The stings were painful and as a resort to rid himself off the little black insects, he sat on the grass and quickly pulled his shoes and stockings. And there they were! Little pieces of paper he had carefully hidden all came out and some were blown away by the wind before he could gather them all.

"What is this?" said the headmaster who stood close by. He picked one of them and read it. "There are some answers here to the quiz" He quickly called back the judges who were already leaving and a brief meeting was held while the pupils trooped back into the school hall, to await the new verdict. When they made their decision, the tall man spoke once more.

"We have discovered that Master Peter has broken the rules of the quiz competition by cheating his opponent. He is therefore disqualified and he is to be severely punished by his school authorities. Master Goodluck is now the winner of the junior category quiz competition" Goodluck's joy knew no bounds as he was ushered to the stage to be congratulated. The judge shook his hand and smiled at him "You will go very far as you continue to tell the truth always. As a compensation for punishing you earlier, we have agreed that your cash prize will be increased from one pound to two pounds. Congratulations! You are a really lucky boy; you should be called Lucky Joe"

Goodluck could not believe his ears. Everyone cheered and applauded loudly "Lucky Joe, Lucky Joe, Lucky Joe". Mr. Olu was right all along. All the pupils congratulated Goodluck and the headmaster received his prizes for safe keeping-two pounds, some textbooks and pencils.

That evening Mr. Olu went to the Jonathan's hut to give his parents the prizes and to tell them what a wonderful son they had. Two pounds was a lot of money and they could pay Goodluck's school fees the next year. Ma Jonathan beamed with pride. Her Goodman had only been in school for a year and he was already putting smiles on their faces.

Pa Jonathan nodded proudly as they listened to Mr. Olu narrate the story from start to finish. "That's my son, that's my boy that's my Lucky Joe" he said over and over again.

CHAPTER 5

Christmas At Grandma Jo's

Story time....

The year 1965 soon reached its end and it was December again, the month when the birth of Jesus is celebrated. Every where in Otuoke people made preparations for the season. They cleaned, cooked, bought new clothes and made merry the best they could. For Goodluck, Christmas time was a whole week of fun at Grandma Jonathan's hut. Grandma Jo-as she was fondly called was his paternal grandmother and she made special preparations for her grand children at Christmas. This year was no exception and after their hut had been decorated and cleaned, Goodluck and Obebatein set out for Grandma Jo's hut which was on the farther end of the village. Benson's parents had allowed him to spend this Christmas with Goodluck, so he joined them. Goodluck and Benson walked a little ahead of Obebatein, chatting about Christmas holidays.

"The best Christmas I ever had was last year when my uncle came to visit" Benson told Goodluck "He bought a fat she-goat with which my mother made the most delicious soup." He gestured with his hands wide apart, to show the size of the goat.

"So, you mean your family finished a whole goat last year Christmas?" Goodluck was surprised because the poor hardly had such a privilege. One chicken at Christmas was great, two or three was splendid, but a whole goat? That was stupendous!

"No" Benson quickly replied "My father would never allow that. Not because the goat wasn't ours to keep but because he loves to share, especially at Christmas. He says it is the true spirit of the season. So Mohammed's family and all the other neighbors had a portion"

"You are right. Even when we don't have much to give at Christmas, my parents make sure Obebatein and I help the old woman who lives next door with some of her chores" Goodluck agreed. They continued to talk on the way until they reached

Grandma Jo's hut. She was expecting them already and sat outside waiting.

"Grandma Jo!" Obebatein called out as they reached the hut. She knelt down to greet her and gave her a hug. Goodluck and Benson followed her example.

"Oh! My children, my dear, dear, children!" Grandma Jo reached out to all of them with her hands, touching their heads and pulling their nose lovingly. She was just as glad to see them as they were to see again. Grandma Jo raised her tall wrinkled frame from the stool where she sat. Now more than eighty years old, she stood a little hunch but despite her age, she was still so strong that her agility remained a mystery to her grand kids. Her eyes held the glow of a youthful flame which danced around when she smiled and her wrinkled skin was still a fine dark brown color; one could easily tell it must have looked liked soft polish leather in her younger days. Grandma Jo inspected them from head to foot.

"Is this not Benson?" she asked as she recognized him.

"Yes, Mama. He has also come to spend Christmas with you" Goodluck replied.

"The last time I saw you, you were this small" She gestured the height with her open palm lowered to the ground. "And Obebatein you are growing into a young lady now" She turned her grand daughter around smiling. Looking at Goodluck, she called him by the name she gave him at his birth "Azikiwe, my own Azikiwe. You are a small man, not so?" She named him after the first president of Nigeria, Dr. Nnamdi Azikiwe, a great leader who fought for the nation's independence from the British rule. All four of them went into the hut and Grandma Jo gave them launch after a cool bathe. She was an excellent cook and she always prepared delicious meals for them at Christmas.

Soon, it was night fall, Goodluck's favorite time of their visit. After a steaming dinner of fresh fish soup and yam, they roasted fish in the small fire grandma Jo made, listening to her stories. They sat under the big tree that stood beside the hut and the three children sat on the ground looking up at her as she recalled wonderful memories of her youth that time could never erase. The moon shone brightly in the pitch dark night sky and the songs of crickets filled the air as grandma began her tales, taking the children on an adventure. She told stories of the lion, king of the animals and the tortoise, the wise creature that lives in a hard shell; of the mighty elephant who uses his long nose for a hand and the little ant who is always busy building his large hilly house of clay. Grandma Jo spoke of the beautiful places she had seen and heard of in her lifetime. The children dreamily travelled with her to the Farin Ruwa waterfalls in Nassarawa State, where lots of water gushed so quickly that it looked like white smoke from afar. This she said, was the reason why the Hausa call it "farin ruwa"meaning white water. She led them on to the deep, mysterious Ebomi Lake in Ondo state on which leaves never fall even though there are many surrounding trees. They listened keenly as she told them of the legendary Queen of Sheba and the Sungbo Eredo site in Ogun state where people believed she was buried. She described the gigantic Olumo rock of Abeokuta and Zuma rock of the Niger which made Goodluck wonder if there was any rock that big.

"Grandma Jo, so the rock looks like gigantic stone bigger than many houses?" He asked in amazement.

"Yes, Azikiwe. It is very big." She replied revealing her brown stained teeth as she smiled.

Obebatein was beginning to nod as the night was far spent by now but like the others she was not ready to go to bed. "Grandma Jo" she said drowsily "can you tell us one of the stories about the great heroes and kings? Please?"

"I must let you go to sleep now. All of nature is resting and so must you" Granma Jo replied.

"Oh but please, Grandma Jo, just this last one" Benson also pleaded.

"Okay, okay. I will tell one last tale about a king named Jaja. He was the ruler of Opobo town, long, long ago..." She began yet another tale of how Jaja rose from being a slave boy at twelve to become one of the most powerful kings of the Niger Delta. The fire was almost out now and the three youngsters fell asleep around the glowing logs and black charcoal, Grandma Jo's voice echoing in their dreams. That night, Goodluck dreamt he was a great hero, who rose out of poverty and became great just like king Jaja.

The rest of the holiday was splendid, and they had the best week ever at Grandma Jo's hut. Even though there was no she-goat slaughtered for the celebration, all three had a very memorable Christmas.

CHAPTER 6

Away from Home

The Jonathans knelt down in their sitting room

G oodluck, are you ready to leave?" Obebatein popped her head into her brother's small room before she walked in.

"Yes" Goodluck replied as he slowly picked up his small sack bag stuffed with his belongings. It was 1967 and time to leave the home he had always known. Mr. Olu has said the government might provide classes four to six at St. Stephen's but it was clear that was not going to happen. Now he was on his way to St. Michael's primary school, Oloibiri to complete his primary education which he started three years ago at St. Stephen's.

"Getting cold feet?" Obebatein asked.

"Maybe. But if I don't go, I wouldn't finish school would I? I am going to miss home" He replied.

"Don't worry. I am coming to take care of you. I am sure we'll be okay at the hut mama rented for us, okay?" she reassured him. Ma Jonathan came in just then.

"My Goodman, I see you are packed and ready"

"Yes mama".

"Your father is in the sitting room. Let's go pray together"

The Jonathans believed strongly in God and the family often prayed together especially in trying moments. Ma Jonathan tried to appear calm but it worried her that her son had to be away from home at a time when things seemed to be fallen apart in the country. The unrest in the North and East had been on over the years and by July 1967; it had grown into a civil war. A senior army officer of the east, Odumegwu Ojukwu had declared the region an independent nation known as the republic of Biafra and this act sparked off the war. It was indeed a time for prayer. The Jonathans knelt down in their sitting room and together, called on God for protection. At the end of the prayer, Pa Jonathan advised his children to be well behaved and careful when ever they met a stranger. Obebatein and Goodluck picked up their bags and began walking to the river where they would board a canoe to

Oloibiri. Benson met them at the river bank to say goodbye to his friends. Goodluck was ahead of him a class, so he could not join him at St. Michael that year.

"I wish you were coming with me" Goodluck said sadly.

He walked to the blackboard and wrote in capital letters "SOCIAL STUDIES"

"I guess I have to study hard so I can join you next year" Benson replied.

"I promise to visit when ever I come to Otuoke" Goodluck placed his bag next to his sister's in the canoe and said goodbye to

Benson. As the ferry man paddled away, Benson waved at them till his arm grew weary, then he headed home. Goodluck watched his friend disappear in the distance as everything in sight grew smaller. Oloibiri was three hours away by canoe and it will be difficult for ten years old Goodluck to go there every day; but as they paddled farther away from Otuoke, Goodluck wished he could come back home everyday.

"Don't feel home sick yet. We've not even left Otuoke" Obebatein studied her brother's mood closely and she took a guess at what he was thinking. He managed a smile as her voice reminded him that he was not alone.

They arrived Oloibiri in a few hours and settled down in their home. Obebatein and Ma Jonathan had already been there a few days earlier to make sure it was ready before they moved in. The hut was just a room with a small wooden window and a door. It was not comfortable but it was all Ma Jonathan could afford and Goodluck was grateful.

The next day, Goodluck woke up early as he always did and began getting ready for school. Everything felt strange and unfamiliar, even the bright yellow sun seemed a little different. Obebatein walked him to school to make sure he didn't miss his way. After an hour's walk, they reached the school and his sister walked back to there rented hut. Goodluck stood at the gate and read the sign board.

"St.Micheal's primary school Oloibiri" He read aloud. Then he joined the assembly in the compound. The pupils were like a multitude to Goodluck who was used to seeing not more than fifteen pupils at an assembly. As they marched off to class, Goodluck surveyed the school compound. There was a large school hall and two other buildings which had three classrooms each, making primary one to six. Soon, lessons began but for the first time since his school days, Goodluck was distracted as he constantly thought of home. He thought of the little pieces of ice that fell from the heavens in the rainy months of May, June and July; they would pick them up and let the cold lumps dissolve in their mouths. In the evening after a heavy downpour, the boys would rush out wearing only shorts and scout for the little fishes which their parents claimed fell from the sky. Goodluck remembered how at night, they went snail hunting to pick the snails that had been hiding from the heat of the sun all day and had now come out in cool of the night. He wished Benson would come to St. Michael's soon. His teacher's voice quickly called back his attention. I am not in Otuoke he thought to himself I am in Oloibiri and I must work hard to complete my studies

Mr. Martins was his class teacher and he was welcoming the new pupils. Each one stood up to introduce himself and Goodluck did the same.

"My name is Goodluck Azikiwe Ebele Jonathan"

"Yes, Mr. Azikiwe. Where are you from?" Mr. Martins smiled.

"Ogbia Local government area, Otuoke village"

"Welcome to Oloibiri. You can sit down. What do you know of Oloibiri?"

"Not much sir, only that it produces lots of oil." Goodluck replied.

"Correct. This is the first place where oil was discovered in large quantity and it produces about 5,100 barrels a day. That's a lot isn't it?"

"Yes Sir" Goodluck replied.

"Apart from that, Oloibiri is a peaceful, wonderful society to live in and speaking of society our first lesson for today is..." He walked to the blackboard and wrote in capital letters "SOCIAL STUDIES"

Goodluck liked his teacher already. He spoke calmly and put everyone at ease. Goodluck also met some nice pupils at school and when the day was done, he had found the cure for home sickness. As he walked home, he moved cheerfully till he reached their hut and he told his sister about his first day at St. Michaels. A few days later, Ade also showed up at Oloibiri. Goodluck was delighted to see him.

"Ade" he happily greeted his classmate from St. Stephen's. "How glad I am to see you"

"I am glad to see you too, Goodluck." Ade replied

"I thought you were going to attend another school"

"Well, here I am. And I'm going to have the first place all through the years here" Ade playfully boasted.

One day at a time took them through their first year at Oloibiri. Ade was good company and they carried on with their academic competition every school term. Goodluck saw Benson whenever he visited Otuoke and he told him all about his new school. By the next year, Benson had joined him at St. Michael's to begin class four. The two friends were happy at their reunion and they studied hard together. Whenever they needed to, they kindled every memory of their home and relived the moments. If they could not be in Otuoke, at least Otuoke was alive in them.

CHAPTER 7

High School Fever

They tattled until they were bored, then raced each other home, splattering rain water pools as they sprinted all the way

Goodluck and Benson walked to school together on a cold Tuesday morning, talking about the mock examination which was coming up in two weeks. They were both seeking for admission into high school and Benson had decided to skip his primary six classes to do so. The mock examination was to prepare them for the entrance examination into high school. Every one in class five and six was talking about it because they were anxious and the teachers never failed to mention it at every opportunity.

"The teachers ring it like a bell" Benson lamented "It seems

Goodluck smiled still gazing at their scores boldly displayed on the school notice board

even a sneeze would make you fail the entrance examination. Mrs. Koi Ko... I mean Mrs. Connery mentions it in like every sentence in our lessons in class. Oh, I wish we'll just be done with it already"

Goodluck laughed aloud, "What was that you called her?"

"You mean Mrs. Koi Koi? That's because of her high heeled shoes that go "Koi koi" on the cemented floors in class. The other pupils nick named her Mrs. Koi Koi and well you know the name stick" Benson replied as he picked some straw grass growing by the road and shot them in the air like arrows.

"Your class is really naughty. She better not hear anyone call her that. And for the exam, if you think you've heard enough, try listening to the sermons all through class five up to six. I can give a lecture about it without blinking. But I think our teachers just want us to do well, that's all" Goodluck picked some grass and joined in his friend's sport.

"You really think so?"

"I know so."

"Well, I guess you're right. Pupils liked us cannot afford to repeat a class. My parents will certainly not pay extra fees"

"I want Mama and Papa to be happy and proud. Mama works so hard and she wants me to go all the way with my education."

"By all the way you mean to the university right? So what will you study?" Benson was excited at the thought of it.

"I think I like animals. I might do something related to that"

"That should be zoology. It's the study of animals. I can see Grandma Jo's lion and tiger stories have got to you." Benson teased.

"Not really" Goodluck replied not wanting to openly admit how much he missed his Grandma's stories.

"I think it will be great to go to the university. But first we have to pass the entrance before we could ever get there. Sometimes, I wonder if we ever will"

"Don't worry, we'll surely get there. We'll just keep studying hard as always" Goodluck assured Benson as they got to class and settled down for another day of academic grooming.

Together, Goodluck and Benson studied hard for and when the mock examination results were ready, they passed in flying colors.

"We did it!" Benson leaped for joy "I knew we would. Mater Dei, here we come!"

Mater Dei was the high school most of the pupils wanted to attend. It was at Imringi town and the entrance examination was to hold there in a week's time.

"If we passed the mock examination here, we will surely do well at Imringi." Goodluck smiled still gazing at their scores boldly displayed on the school notice board.

Just then, Ade walked up to meet them where they stood. "I see you have seen the mock results." He said "You outdid me this time, Goodluck. You did great too, Benson. So, you are skipping class six?"

"Thank you, yes I am" Benson replied proudly as skipping a class meant was a mark of intelligence.

"So which high school would you like to attend? Asked Goodluck

"Mater Dei." Ade replied "You?"

"Same"

"I guess you guys will continue your academic competition there right?" Benson laughed.

"We'll see about that!" Ade smiled as he skipped off.

Goodluck and Benson talked about high school on their way home – Their expectations, their dreams and the good life after graduation. They spoke of how they would get the best jobs so they could support their families. Their mothers would never sell fish at the market and their fathers would no longer labour so hard at farms to feed the home. They even dreamt of how they would change the whole country. It was 1969, the time when the civil war was at its peak and the common people suffered. People were afraid to go to farms and some were starving. Some of Goodluck's colleagues had even dropped out of school but he and Benson were determined to go on.

"After I'm educated, I will tell Nigerians not to fight anymore. I know they'll listen because I'll be a graduate then. I believe I can change a lot of things when I grow up." Goodluck said passionately.

"You know, when you talk like this, I feel like you are going to be very important someday" Benson told him

"Me? I just want to help people that's all."

"Well, Mrs. Koi... I mean Mrs. Connery tells us in class that a helping hand is owned by a great man. As for the war, Papa told me it will soon be over. That was last month when we visited Otuoke."

"Speaking of visit, we are supposed to visit Otuoke this weekend. How could I have forgotten?" Goodluck sounded excited. He loved visiting home.

"You forgot because of the high school examination fever going round" Benson teased.

"No, I did not have exam fever" Goodluck objected.

"Yes, you did" Benson insisted.

"I did not"

"You did"

"Did not"

"Did"

They tattled on till they were bored, then raced each other home, splattering rain water pools, as they sprinted all the way.

CHAPTER 8

Goodluck THE CANOE CARVER

Papa why don't I help you with your carving, you work so hard and I want to help you

Goodluck and Benson awaited the results of the Mater Dei entrance examination, at home in Otuoke. Goodluck was not worried about his performances because he did his very best. But he wondered how his parents would cope with his school fees when he got into high school. The Jonathans had been affected by the war like everyone else and their poor condition had grown worse. Ma Jonathan's fish trade was not going as well as it used to and Pa Jonathan was doing all he could with the canoe carving. Goodluck wished there was something he could do to help. Ma Jonathan assured her son that all would be well and he believed her. But the news on radio made Goodluck ask a lot of questions.

"Papa, if Nigeria wins the war against Biafra, the country will be one again, right?"

"Yes" Pa Jonathan replied without looking up from his work. He was at his small work space adding finishing touches to a canoe he had carved. Goodluck sat on a small log of wood, watching his father.

"Then everything will be okay and things won't be bad anymore?" He continued his questions.

"That's right. Hand me that planer tool beside you" Pa Jonathan said stretching out his left hand to collect it.

"But what if Nigeria doesn't win?" Goodluck handed his father the tool. Pa Jonathan stopped for a moment and looked at his son.

"You worry about things far bigger than you. Leave the worrying to the older folk, okay? Everything will sort itself out. And besides, there are rumours that the war will soon be over and there will be peace" Pa Jonathan assured Goodluck.

"Really? That will be wonderful" Goodluck smiled at the sound of the word "peace". All he had heard grown ups talk about was danger but peace sounded better. Goodluck concentrated on watching his father carve. Then, he had a brilliant idea. Why, he could help his father carve. He had watched it done several times;

They scrambled onto the boat to paddle but fell into the water instead with a big splash

he felt he could even carve a canoe all by himself.

"Papa, why don't I help you with your carving? You work so hard and I want to help" Goodluck quickly offered.

Pa Jonathan wiped the sweat from his forehead, laughing

heartily. "You? Carve? As little as you are, I wonder if you would carve the wood or the wood would carve you!" He returned to his task.

Goodluck meant what he said and he pestered his father everyday, until he grew weary of his request. Pa Jonathan gave him a small log of wood and Goodluck set to work. Everyday, when his father worked, he joined him and followed what he did carefully. It was hard work and Goodluck had many cuts and bruises to show for it but he was determined to finish what he started. He worked with an adze, a small axe, a planner and knife.

One day, Benson came to visit and met his friend carving. "Ah, Goodluck what are you up to? See how you are sweating!" Benson exclaimed.

"What does it look like? I'm carving so I can help Papa" He replied as he looked up from his work and smiled.

"That work is way too much and you haven't got huge muscles for it" Benson laughed

"Who says? My father is canoe carver and I'm his son. It runs in the family." Goodluck returned to his work.

Benson watched him work for a while and gave him a helping hand. Pa Jonathan came back from his break to find two carvers instead of one.

"Oho! Who is this? Benson. You are carving too?"

"Good afternoon Sir" Benson greeted. "He can't do it alone, so I'm helping"

"I tried to discourage him but he remained adamant, so I gave him that to work with. Anyway, it's good to have courage to try things out; even failure is a stepping stone to success"

Goodluck carved all through the holiday with Benson helping out whenever he could. Finally, a small scrawny canoe emerged. Pa Jonathan, Benson and Goodluck towered over the little thing the afternoon it was finished admiring it. It wasn't a fine boat but Pa Jonathan felt proud that his twelve year old had made such a bold attempt just to help him. Goodluck and Benson were excited about their work and they couldn't wait to try it out too. Together, they dragged it to the river bank and pushed it into the water.

"It floats" Goodluck said delightfully.

"Let's get in and paddle!" said Benson lifting a small paddle in the air.

They scrambled onto the boat to paddle but fell into the water instead with a big splash! Being excellent swimmers, they swam to land pulling the canoe after them. Benson was the first to burst into laughter and Goodluck joined him. When they were calmer, the duo turned the small boat aright and pushed it back into the river with only Goodluck in it.

"Well, if doesn't work, don't feel too bad. Remember your father said failure is sometimes a stepping stone to success" Benson assured his friend as the boat wobbled a little. "Sit carefully so it remains steady. Okay, now paddle!" He instructed

Goodluck sat down and paddled away happily, waving at his friend.

"All hail the canoe carver!" Benson shouted out to his friend.

Suddenly, Ade ran to where Benson stood, glowing with excitement. Goodluck watched him talk with Benson but he could not hear them properly. He paddled in their direction and when he was within earshot, Ade blurted out marvelous news.

"My father saw our results at Mater Dei, and we made it!"

Although Goodluck knew already that he would pass, he was still so glad at the news that he jumped up in his boat with his hands held high. Down he went into the water again with a bigger splash than the first. They all laughed together and his friends hailed him as the greatest canoe maker ever.

CHAPTER 9

SHOES FOR Goodluck

Who are you? He asked, his face was rumpled from years of frowning though he was young

Goodluck was excited about his admission into Mater Dei high school and he carefully prepared everything he would need. It was a boarding school and his mother had a list of the necessary items for each student. It was a sunny afternoon and Goodluck was in his room going over the items his mother had bought for him from the market. He turned everything out of the bag and set them aside one by one. "Everything else is here except my shoes." He thought aloud "Mama must have forgotten to buy shoes for me." Goodluck packed up everything neatly, and went to the backyard where his mother and Obebatein sat picking some beans. Goodluck greeted them and sat down to help with the work. When they were done, Obebatein took the beans to their small outdoor kitchen. "Mama" Goodluck called his mother softly.

"Yes, my Goodman" Ma Jonathan replied smiling "What would you like me to do for you?" she knew right away when he wanted something.

"Thank you again for all the things you bought for school. But I think you forgot to buy a pair of shoes"

Ma Jonathan's smile slowly vanished; she looked at her son sadly "I'm sorry, but the shoes were too expensive and I had no money left" She reached out to pat his head but Goodluck did not feel comforted. He desperately wanted those shoes because they were one of the requirements at Mater Dei School. All through his primary school days, he went to school barefooted but he could not do that at high school as well. He hoped something would be done before the following week when he would be leaving for Imringi.

The days went by and soon it was time to leave for school; still there were no shoes for Goodluck. One day, Ade came to visit him and he learnt that Goodluck wasn't going to Mater Dei the next day as planned, because he had no shoes. He quickly offered to lend him an old pair of rubber slippers which he no longer used.

"I know it isn't much" said Ade as he handed the pair to Goodluck. "But he still wasn't happy, though he tired not to show it. On the morning of his departure, he packed all he needed and reluctantly put on the slippers Ade gave him. His parents gave him lots of advice for which he thanked them; Obebatein and Ma Jonathan escorted him to the river where Benson and Ade were already waiting. Before they left in the ferry, Ma Jonathan spoke to her son.

"I know you still want your shoes and I really wanted you to have them. My son, please manage. God will provide. You hear? Please be a good boy" she hugged him and the ferry man paddled away. Obebatein and Ma Jonathan waved goodbye for a while, then turned to leave.

The first weeks at Mater Dei were the worst ever for Goodluck. On arrival, the security guard was the first to harass him with questions. He was ill mannered and rash, none of them liked him.

"Who are you?" I mean you" He pointed at Goodluck "Are you a student here? Why are you not well dressed? Where are your shoes?"

Goodluck was about to explain but the security guard wouldn't let him. He simply flung the gate open.

"You can explain to the principal and teachers. It's not my business really"

As they walked past him, a student whispered to Goodluck. "He's a little ill tempered, but he's nice once you're used to him" He's was a form two student returning from the holiday break.

"Doesn't mean he should be so rude and stupid" Said Ade

Never insult an elder, even when he's wrong" Benson quickly corrected him.

"Hope the teachers won't mind my slippers" Goodluck told the form two students. "I hope to get shoes later"

"Who knows? Maybe they won't since you are new" He replied. But that was not the case, because the teacher did mind. Even his classmate made fun of his slippers and the reason why wasn't far fetched; the ugly slippers were worn out and looked liked they could give out anytime. Goodluck felt embarrassed and sad despite Benson's efforts to cheer him up.

"Maybe we could switch footwear just for today Benson once told him.

But Goodluck only replied "Thank you but then everyone would know that I borrowed them and they'll make fun of me"

One weekend, Obebatein came to visit. Goodluck was glad to see her again and asked a million questions about home.

"How is Mama?" He inquired.

"She's fine"

"Papa and the canoe he was carving before I left"

Both fine"

"And you?"

"As you can see, I'm fine" Obebatein smiled.

"And the pumpkin vegetables I planted near the kitchen. How are they?" Obebatein laughed aloud. "You are asking about that too? Well, I've cooked and eaten them, so I can tell you they were fine in the dish" She asked Goodluck if he liked his new school and they talked about it for a while.

Mater Dei is great. But I still miss home. You are not here with me as you were in Oloibiri" he said.

"Anything else?" Obebatein raised an eye brow expectantly.

Goodluck paused for a moment and looked down at the ugly pair of slippers on his feet. "Everyone in class makes fun of my slippers. The principals asked why I didn't have them, and said I should go home if I don't get them soon. I feel really bad about it and I still need a new pair of..." He stopped talking as he lifted his head because in front of him were the most handsome pair of shoes he ever saw.

"Sister Obebatein! Thank you! They are wonderful!" Goodluck's joy knew no bounds.

"You have Papa to thank for them he felt so bad that you were going to school in those slippers. You remember that little canoe you carved over the holidays?" Goodluck nodded that he did. "Papa worked on it again and made it really pretty. He took it all the way to the next village and managed to sell it there. Maybe it's a reward for working so hard"

Goodluck quickly took off his footwear and put on his new

shoes. Before Obebatein returned to Otuoke, Goodluck told her to tell Pa Jonathan how grateful he was. When he got to the hostel, he showed Benson his new shoes.

"Wow!" Benson exclaimed "Those are shoes! Let's see our classmates tease you now"

Indeed, no one teased him anymore and teachers praised him for his sharp appearance. Even the security guard passed him a good compliment. Goodluck was glad that the embarrassment was finally over. But Goodluck's new shoes were just an introduction to good news to come, because by the Christmas of 1969, the war was nearly over. The head of state of Biafra, Lt. Col. Odumegwu Ojukwu fled to the Ivory coast and so the 14th of January 1970, saw the end of a bitter war. The news spread quickly through Nigeria and there was a great joy and jubilation. Goodluck's return to school that January after the Christmas holidays marked the beginning of the best school days he ever had. They were spent in peace, free from the strife that war brings.

CHAPTER 10

RISE OF A LEADER

Goodluck's hostel mates ran towards him excitedly and lifted him shoulder high

It was a Wednesday afternoon at Mater Dei School; the students had just concluded lessons and were headed for the hostels, when the school bell rang loudly. The sound echoed in the large school compound, breaking the silence. Goodluck and Benson were already at the gate of their hostel, when they heard it.

"Oooh! Who could be ringing that bell at this time?" Asked an exhausted Benson who still felt a slight headache he got from solving math on a hot afternoon. It was siesta time and the bell was a huge interruption.

"Maybe there's an announcement" Goodluck said dusting his new pair of trousers with his white handkerchief. They were now in form four class and wore trousers and long sleeve shirts instead of the usual short sleeve and short. "You know nap time could be announcement time, sometimes" he laughed.

"Well, I don't like it. Why do we have a math class in the afternoon anyway? Mr. Class prefect?" Benson queried his friend as they made a U-turn and walked towards the school hall.

"You know, I've thought of talking to the math teacher about it" Goodluck replied. He was appointed as the class prefect in form three because of his brilliant performance at school and his good example of keeping all school rules. He had not wanted the position but their form teacher insisted firmly. Shortly after, he was also appointed as the secretary of the Mater Dei food committee. Goodluck didn't like the spot light but it seemed to always find him out.

"When you were first made class prefect, I thought you may not take it seriously because you didn't want it. But look at you now, you do your job so well" Benson commended him.

"I can still hand you the position, if you like" Goodluck replied smiling.

"No, Goodluck, you're the man. The great canoe carver, true son of his father, class prefect and secretary of the food committee" Benson teased and they both laughed aloud. As they approached the hall, they saw some of their colleagues walking to

Ma Jonathan watched the event with tears in her eyes as she saw her little Goodman, now eighteen throw his graduation cap in the air alongside his colleagues...

the hostel.

"Where are you going?" Goodluck asked them

"To get some sleep, of course. If we hide under the bed, no one will find us. I'm too tired man" One of them replied. Goodluck said nothing more as they passed on but he was not happy with their behavior. He did not like it when student broke school rules.

"Why won't they just do the right thing?" He questioned no one in particular.

"They better thank their lucky stars that I'm not Masterson house prefect" There were many hostels in the school known as houses and Masterson house was the name of Goodluck and Benson's hostel.

"I think you maybe appointed for just that" Benson said.

"No, it's just a thought. How can I find time to handle that position? My studies would suffer and that is what I'm really here for. I can't afford to repeat one class." Goodluck replied as they stepped into the hall. The principal was already on the platform speaking to the students and they noticed some students were standing beside him. They walked to a desk and were barely seated, when Goodluck heard his name.

"The new Masterson house prefect is Goodluck Ebele Jonathan" It was the principal who called him and all the students applauded loudly.

Goodluck remained rooted to his seat, trying to make sense of the scene playing out before him. He slowly stood up and began walking to the platform, while the principal called up other students. Ade's name was also called but Goodluck did not hear him because he was still dazed to listen. House prefect? This is definitely the biggest distraction from school work. Goodluck thought as he climbed the stairs to the stage. When the assembly was dismissed, Goodluck went to see the principal in his office to tell him he couldn't accept the position.

"Why?" The principal asked. He cleaned his glasses with a piece of cloth as he spoke. "I am sure you are more than competent for the position. Why do you refuse?"

"Sir, I do not mean to doubt your good judgment, but I do not want any distractions from my studies"

Goodluck replied.

"Distraction? This is not a distraction; it is part of your education. Learning is not just in the class room you know. It is training for tomorrow's leaders like you. You seem not to like leadership but you are very good at it. Your form teacher told me of your initial refusal to be class prefect. But you see how well you do the work"

"But sir..."

"No buts. Mr. Goodluck, you are the new Masterson house prefect, period." The principal said with finality as he put on his glasses. This meant that the conversation was over and Goodluck quietly left the office.

All through the next week, Goodluck was pressured by teachers and colleagues to accept the position, until he reluctantly gave in. Benson was happy with his friend's new position and he congratulated him.

"Hey, congrats! I always said you were the man!" He said as he gave Goodluck a friendly pat on the back. "Its just that you'll need a lot of wisdom to lead this bunch"

"I think I have a little and I hope it will do" Goodluck replied

"Well, you could borrow some more from Ade, he is the new house prefect of wisdom house, so he should have plenty"

Goodluck laughed at the joke, "I'll do just that"

But he did have a lot of wisdom at hand, so much that the rebellious students of the Masterson house were soon tamed under his gentle but firm leadership. The hostel became the neatest as it became compulsory for everyone to do their sanitation exercise. Even Benson was not left out as there were no preferences or special treatments. Though it was hard and tiresome at first, it was worth it in the end. All the students obeyed school rules because Goodluck would not tolerate rule breaking. Masterson house also became the best in sports. The students had been known for coming at the last position at sports activities but Goodluck encouraged all athletes to nurse their talents diligently. He told them they could do better and he expected a gold trophy from their efforts. Though he preferred to read always, he volunteered to play table tennis to encourage them and they were happy to see him sweat it out with them on the court. At the next inter-house sports, Masterson house was at the first position with Wisdom house close on their heels as second position. The principal smiled broadly as he handed the gold trophy to Goodluck on behalf of his hostel.

"I knew you would do well, my boy! You are a true leader. You will surely be great in future." He shook Goodluck's hand vigorously.

"Thank you sir" He replied.

Goodluck's hostel mates ran to him excitedly and lifted him shoulder high, happily chanting as they carried him around the school field.

We are the best!

Better than the rest!

Our leader is the champ!

So come and join our camp!

Goodluck continued to lead his hostel in victory, till he got to form six when it was time to graduate from high school. All the Masterson house students loved him dearly and wish he would remain with them. But still, they were happy that he had completed his studies at Mater Dei and was now moving ahead.

On the graduation day, everyone was in attendance- students, parents, teachers and well wishers. The Jonathans and Agadagas' sat side by side in the section reserved for parents and they watched with pride as their sons were called up to receive awards for making a distinction in their studies. Goodluck was also awarded for outstanding leadership in his years as house prefect. Ma Jonathan watched the event with tears in her eyes as she saw her little Goodman now eighteen, throw his graduation cap in the air along side his colleagues in celebration of their achievement. Pa Jonathan was also proud of his son and he was glad he let him go to school. The long struggle for education was worth it in the end; for the Otuoke village boy was now on his rise to greatness.

Epilogue

...a five year old girl named Uwethu knew the presidents declaration speech by heart and she was there to memorize another

Goodluck looked through the tinted window of the limousine car as it drove to the eagle square, Abuja. Everyone knew he was going to be great someday, but no one guessed just how great he would be because his was flawless flight from grass to grace. Thirty five years later, he was the number one citizen of the federal republic of Nigeria. He was first the deputy governor of Bayelsa State and a few years later, the governor of the state. By 2007, he was sworn in as the vice president of Nigeria and now, it was May 29th 2011, the day he would be sworn in as president of the country for the next four years. For a while, it was like a dream; the past years were still too real and fresh in his memory- Otuoke village, the poverty and his struggle to attend school. As they zoomed past the buildings of Abuja city, he recalled his childhood days as though each building was a memory they left behind. He had seen some of the beautiful places grandma Jo always spoke about and the Zuma rock which was a mystery to him then was so close to Abuja where he lived. Numerous voices which had prophesied of his greatness in the past now bounced back into his ears. Grandma Jo had always called him Azikiwe, after the great Zik of Africa and Benson's small voice at twelve had said I feel like you are going to be very important someday.

When they got to the eagle square and the ceremony began, there were all sorts of people to be seen in the crowd. Citizens had traveled from far and near to grace the swearing in of the first president to come from the Niger Delta. Little children came with their parents from all over the country to be inspired by a great man. Musa who was an eight year old from Plateau State was present with his older sister Aisha and her husband Emeka.

"Uncle Emeka" Musa said "I want to be a great man when I grow up like President Jonathan "

"Well, you surely can" Uncle Emeka smiled at him. "If you could work hard as he did, he wasn't born with a silver spoon but look where he is today"

"So you mean if he did it, I can do it too?"

"Exactly! My smart boy!" Uncle Emeka replied as he gave him a high five.

A five year old girl named Uwethu knew the president's declaration speech by heart and she was there at the eagle square to memorize another. President Jonathan was her ultimate hero and she was going to recite his inauguration speech in a school play at home in Ahoada, Rivers State. As the president spoke, she repeated every word in whisper from where she sat beside her mother. When he said his last words, she was already asleep on her mother's lap. But as she slept, she had a beautiful vision were she saw a better Nigeria with patriotic leaders and citizens, and in that dream, one of those leaders was Uwethu.

GOODLUCK JONATHAN'S DECLARATION SPEECH
18 September 2010 14:42

Forty months ago my predecessor in office and I embarked on a joint ticket in the governance of our great country, Nigeria. Sadly, he passed away on the 5th of May 2010.

MAY HIS GENTLE SOUL REST IN PERFECT PEACE, AMEN.

With the death of President Umaru Musa Yar'Adua, the mantle of leadership of our great nation fell on me. However, the days leading to my presidency were very trying times for our nation. We confronted those moments and their challenges to national security with patriotism and care. I appreciate the role played by the National Assembly, Governors, Civil Society groups, the mass media, and other patriotic Nigerians.

The late President Yar'Adua and I shared great dreams for our country. We toiled together to realize those dreams in order to justify the confidence Nigerians reposed in us. Together we swore to execute a joint mandate and today I come before you to make a pronouncement based on that undertaking.

The past four months that I have served as President of Nigeria have opened my eyes to the vast potentials of this office as a potent instrument for the transformation of our country. I discovered that by sheer willpower, I could end the long queues and price fluctuations in our petrol stations. Today, all our refineries are working, saving us huge amounts of funds spent on importation of petroleum products.

I discovered that by insisting that the right things be done, we could begin a turnaround in our power sector by involving the private sector in power generation and distribution. As you can see from the lower quantities of diesel that you are buying today, power generation has significantly improved.

I have put in place new gas policies and very soon, we will be saying goodbye to gas flaring in our oil fields. Working with the National Assembly, we rolled out a law that requires companies operating in the oil and gas sectors of our economy to utilize an appreciable percentage of their goods and services from local sources. We saw to it that normalcy began to return to the Niger Delta by ensuring government's fidelity to its promises, and this has helped to stabilize our national revenue.

In the last few months, I embarked on monumental projects in our road infrastructure to end the carnage on our federal highways. I began several projects to make our water resources available for drinking and farming. I targeted our educational system to return quality and competitiveness to them. I re-addressed our drive for self sufficiency in food production. I have taken bold steps to confront our security situation. In this regard, we are pursuing the revision of our laws to be more responsive to international conventions and more punitive to criminals.

I set the stage for free and fair elections by constituting an electoral commission comprising of Nigerians with impeccable credentials for firmness and incorruptibility. I charged our anti corruption agencies to speed up the war against corruption, and respect no sacred cows in the process. In the management of the economy, I advocated a more transparent banking industry, price stability, low inflation, and aggregate increase in productivity as a way to drive us to a more prosperous economy. In International Relations, I advanced the respectability accorded our country by effective engagement in global fora.

From the moment I was sworn in as President, I came under intense pressure to make a declaration concerning my political future, but declined to do so because it would have immediately distracted us from all the development initiatives we have accomplished so far.

As President and leader of this government, I decided not to place partisan politics above the immediate needs and priorities of our people. I therefore told Nigerians to give me time to concentrate on my work, and that at the appropriate time, I would make a public statement on my political future after widespread consultations.

Those consultations have now been concluded. The Independent National Electoral Commission has recently announced a time table for the 2011 general elections in the country. My party, the Peoples Democratic Party, has also published a timetable for its primaries.

In the circumstances and after a thorough self examination and prayers with my family, I, Goodluck Ebele Azikiwe Jonathan have decided to humbly offer myself as a candidate in the Presidential Primaries of our great party, the Peoples Democratic Party, in order to stand for the 2011 Presidential elections. I pledge once again to all the people of this nation that they will have a free and fair election, even as I stand to be a candidate. In this race, I have the honour to have as my running mate, Architect Namadi Sambo, the Vice President of the Federal Republic of Nigeria.

Our country is at the threshold of a new era; an era that beckons for a new kind of leadership; a leadership that is uncontaminated by the prejudices of the past; a leadership committed to change; a leadership that reinvents government, to solve the everyday problems that confront the average Nigerian.

I was not born rich, and in my youth, I never imagined that I would be where I am today, but not once did I ever give up. Not once did I imagine that a child from Otuoke, a small village in the Niger Delta, will one day rise to the position of President of the Federal Republic of Nigeria. I was raised by my mother and father with just enough money to meet our daily needs.

In my early days in school, I had no shoes, no school bags. I carried my books in my hands but never despaired; no car to take me to school but I never despaired. There were days I had only one meal but I never despaired. I walked miles and crossed rivers to school every day but I never despaired. Didn't have power, didn't have generators, studied with lanterns but I never despaired.

In spite of these, I finished secondary school, attended the University of Port Harcourt, and now hold a doctorate degree.

Fellow Nigerians, if I could make it, you too can make it!

My story is the story of a young Nigerian whose access to education opened up vast opportunities that enabled me to attain my present position. As I travel up and down our country, I see a nation blessed by God with rich agricultural and mineral resources and an enterprising people. I see millions of Nigerians whose potentials for greatness are constrained by the lack of basic infrastructure.

I see Nigerians who can make a difference in the service of their country but are disadvantaged by the lack of opportunities.

My story symbolizes my dream for Nigeria. The dream that any Nigerian child from Kaura- Namoda to Duke town; from Potiskum to Nsukka, from Isale-Eko to Gboko will be able to realize his God-given potentials, unhindered by tribe or religion and unrestricted by improvised political inhibitions. My story holds out the promise of a new Nigeria. A Nigeria built on the virtues of love and respect for one another, on unity, on industry, on hard-work and on good governance.

My fellow Nigerians, this is what has brought me to Eagle Square today. I have come to say to all of you, that Goodluck Ebele Azikiwe Jonathan is the man you need to put Nigeria right. I have come to launch a campaign of ideas, not one of calumny. I have come to preach love, not hate. I have come to break you away from divisive tendencies of the past which have slowed our drive to true nationhood. I have no enemies to fight. You are all my friends and we share a common destiny.

Let the word go out from this Eagle Square that Jonathan as President in 2011 will herald a new era of transformation of our country; an era that will end the agony of power shortage in our country. Let the word go out from here that I will be for the students, teachers and parents of Nigeria, a President who will advance quality and competitive education. Let everyone in this country hear that I shall strive to the best of my ability to attain self sufficiency in food production.

Let the word go out that my plans for a Sovereign Wealth Fund with an initial capital of $1billion will begin the journey for an economic restoration. This restoration will provide new job opportunities and alleviate poverty. Let the word go out that our health sector will receive maximum priority in a new Jonathan administration, a priority that will ensure maximum health care and stop our brain drain.

Let all the kidnappers, criminal elements, and miscreants that give us a bad name be ready for the fight that I shall give them. Let the ordinary Nigerian be assured that President Jonathan will have zero tolerance for corruption. Let the international community hear that today I have offered myself to lead a country that will engage them in mutual respect and cooperation for the achievement of international peace and understanding.

To help me in these tasks effectively, I will re-train, revamp, and motivate the civil service.

My dear good people of Nigeria, I got here today by the power of

God and the support of all Nigerians; all ethnic groups, North, South, East and West. I am here today because of your support and prayers. I want all of you to know that I am one of you and I will never let you down! I want you to know that I will keep hope alive; I want you to know that your time has come.

I stand before you today, humbly seeking your support for me, Goodluck Ebele Azikiwe Jonathan, to run for the office of the President of Nigeria with Architect Namadi Sambo as my running mate.

We will fight for JUSTICE!

We will fight for all Nigerians to have access to POWER!
We will fight for qualitative and competitive EDUCATION!

We will fight for HEALTH CARE REFORMS!

We will fight to create jobs, for all Nigerians!

We will fight corruption!

We will fight to protect all Citizens!

We will fight for your rights!

My dear country men and women, give me your support, give me your votes and together we will fight to build a great nation of our dreams!

I cannot end this speech without thanking you all for attending this occasion. Your huge attendance is a loud testimony of your support for us. For this I am very grateful. I pray that the Almighty God abides with you and sees you safely back to your respective destinations.

When you return, tell all those at home that as we celebrate our fifty years anniversary as a nation, Goodluck has come to transform Nigeria and I will never let you down.

Thank You.

May God Bless you all!

And may God bless the Federal Republic of Nigeria!!

- GOODLUCK EBELE AZIKIWE JONATHAN, GCFR.